D1557851

salmonpoetry

Publishing Irish & International
Poetry Since 1981

Carlos Reyes

Along the Flaggy Shore

Poems from West Clare

Published in 2018 by
Salmon Poetry
Cliffs of Moher, County Clare, Ireland
Website: www.salmonpoetry.com
Email: info@salmonpoetry.com

Copyright © Carlos Reyes, 2018

ISBN 978-1-912561-35-3

All rights reserved. No part of this publication may be reproduced or transmitted in
any form or by any means, electronic or mechanical, including photography,
recording, or any information storage or retrieval system, without permission in
writing from the publisher. The book is sold subject to the condition that it shall not,
by way of trade or otherwise, be lent, resold or otherwise circulated without the
publisher's prior consent in any form of binding or cover other than that in which it is
published and without a similar condition, including this condition, being imposed on
the subsequent purchaser.

Cover & frontispiece photography: Jessie Lendennie
Cover Design & Typesetting: *Siobhán Hutson*
Printed in Ireland by Sprint Print

And some time make the time to drive out west
Into County Clare, along the Flaggy Shore,
In September or October, when the wind
And the light are working off each other

—SEAMUS HEANEY
"Postscript"

Acknowledgements

I would like to thank the writers, editors, and friends who have encouraged and supported me through my writing years: Christopher Howell, Christine Holbert, Lisa Steinman, Henry Hughes and of course my in-house editor, Karen Checkoway.

I am particularly grateful to the Lafferty Family of Letterkelly who have inspired me over the past forty years.

I would be remiss if I did not acknowledge Ger Killeen, of Limerick, Ireland and Neskowin Oregon, whose expertise on things Irish I have resorted to for almost thirty years.

My especial gratitude to Jessie Lendennie and Siobhán Hutson for taking on this book.

"The Tenants of the World" first appeared in *Reckless Writing* anthology 2013 (Chatter House Press). The poem is also in *Laurel Review*'s issue on immigration.

To Karen, always

Contents

Stolen Song   11

I.   Moonless County Roads   15

     Matins   16

     Michael Niall   17

     Bog Angel   18

     Vigil   20

     The Plough   21

     Three Shadows   23

     Aggie Cleary's   25

     Regret   27

II.   Across the Distance   31

     The Bard at Eighty   32

     Never In Step With What Escaped Me   33

     Here, Again   34

     Keeping Time   36

     "Sea-Sand"   37

     Through the Back Window of Lost Time   38

III. The Tenants of the World   41
      Achill Island   42
      The Deserted Village   43
      Mass Grave Near Ennistymon, Co. Clare   44
      Killaspuglonane   45
      Nightboat   47
      Ballygowan   48

IV.   Trespass   53
      Tottenham's Trees   54
      According to Pakie Russell   55
      A Clare Story   57
      Life, and a Pine Marten   58
      Memory Stone   61
      A Song for St. Paddy's   62

About the author   65

Stolen Song

—after the 14th Century Irish

I am of County Clare
that lovely county

When I am grown a man
fair maid of Quilty

To the Crosses of Annagh
come I beg thee

In name of charity
come dance with me

I

Moonless County Roads

As though we are crossing
a continent or the great American desert
instead of travelling 17 short miles
uphill from Ennis to Letterkelly.

Once you are inside this postage stamp
island and get to know it
you become lost in a much larger world
and no longer care how vast
the sky or the outside world is.

Tonight as we take the sharp bends
the narrow road embraces us, gathers
around our shoulders like a comforting
old wool coat on a rainy night.

As we travel up its dark tunnel—
Fáilte the old road says—we
feel welcomed, at home again.

Matins

No sound, no
traffic on the county road.

No morning
church bells tolling,

tolling Cloonanaha.

Nor cow,
no sound

save the
coo-coo's

counting
reminding,

reminding us
of waning days.

Michael Niall

His parents gone for decades
he too, was gone, submerged
in years he scarce remembers.

Now even drink has forsaken him
but he's floated to the surface
from dark seas of porter.

His legacy has turned to
perfect stillness and flags
of Liscannor stone.

They'd need a bit
of brushing to bring up
the shine, he says,

like himself returned
from a gloom ink black
as the stones he walks.

But his face brightens
the long dead hearth
where we sit talking.

I was hard put
to recognize the shining face
when he came to the door.

It's so quiet out here
down at the end
of the boreen—difficult

to fathom how he lives,
imagine how he saves
the hours or kills them.

Bog Angel

Though more literate than most
he never read the *Book of Daniel*,
nor knew about Susanna and the Elders.
Never saw the paintings,

this old bachelor farmer
who has gone behind the shed.
As he starts to unbutton, he freezes,
breath caught by what he spies

from his vantage through the trees.
Sunbathing nude by the hedge,
Benton's *Persephone*, all marble
white flesh—nakedness

he never witnessed even in dream.
He covers himself before such a vision
but his eyes brighten, devour
every inch of that body sent down

to him from the heavens
as he fumbles through the buttons.
In all his years never saw in the dark
back bedroom such a miracle.

There was no marriage bed
for him, sex was animal husbandry.
The cow no beauty, nor the bull
as it plunged its pike into its mad mate.

But there was an erotic daintiness,
in the carefully wrapped mare's tail
bandaged for the violent coming
together of her and the raging stallion,

Today when it happened—better
had it been the dream come true
years back when he found the woman,
though fully clothed, asleep

on his doorstep. Now he waits,
slow his coming . . . Then
she is gone—that carnal vision—back
into the doorway dark.

Vigil

A semi-circle of candle stones
left an unexplained vigil

in the hearth of my own cottage
long abandoned, or should it be

in my heart, so close the two, but
more, surely, in what I say than

a slip of the tongue, more
than a letter dropped. . .

All of that hovers
as I place a half circle of chairs

at Mary's hearth, await evening
guests, Pa' and Mary to return

from the gloom to join us
at the turf fire, this night dark

as the Liscannor flags I pace,
before I walk outside

for headlights descending
the boreen, search

for a break in the clouds,
for the reassuring Plough.

The Plough

As the sun goes down
the ploughman raises his head,

comes in from the half bog, half grass
stoney field,

wipes the sweat from his brow
with a rag of a kerchief.

After tea he stands before the hearth,
expecting some portent

to rise from the boiling pot,
before he turns, walks out,

looks up for a sign of weather.

What he sees in the north sky
brings from deep inside him

*Why do you torment me when
I'm just after leaving you in the field?*

The ploughman the first
to draw that image in the sky

but afraid to curse God's creation
of eternal labor as the rest intone

God bless the work! the work
that pursues him as long as there is light.

Instead he prays for a blinding
fog to smother the image.

He pushes it from his mind
before he retires for the night,

hides it away in the out buildings
like an old rusty appliance.

Even as he drifts into sleep
the icon rises ever higher, above

four fields yet to plough.

Three Shadows

Standing on the mud-like bank,
I try and fail

to cut the perfect sod of turf.
Pa' says "Not to worry,

sure, and 'tis only a bit o' earth."

That was forty years ago.
Pa' is in that earth now

and nobody cuts turf in the peat bog,
though there's plenty still. Easier
to buy briquettes at the shop in Miltown.

Paddy the son no longer
lives there. I am gone too, far

away from Letterkelly.

Three shadows I see: Pa',
the giant wiping his brow,

Paddy leaning on the slane, me
still trying to get the hang of it.

One by one the old fellas
disappear from the bogs,

from the hay meadows,
from the pubs, but I see them still.

Now I am a shadow
over Paddy, now I am the elder

of a family I share no
blood with

but have been part of
for half my life.

Now
I am the keeper of his family stories,

of his townland Letterkelly,
for him, for me.

Aggie Cleary's

Across a street shining
from morning rain
off Mal Bay, a short woman

in grey takes advantage of a break
in the weather, bends to touch up
the brown door of Cleary's pub.

As I cross to the familiar looking person
she straightens, brightens, turns to me
as I venture, "Grand day."

"Tis," she returns. I ask
"Do you know Aggie Cleary?

"Indeed I do, for she was my mother
I'm the nun. . ." she smiles.

"Many's the pint I drank in her pub," I say

She nods. "Ah, the pub's been closed for ages. . .
"Would ye like to come in?"

    Glasses are washed and rinsed,
    stacked neat as ricks of turf,
    glittering trapezoids ready still.

    Aggie dusts the padded bench
    along the wall in anticipation.
    I am there after forty years

    breathing the same stale
    smell of porter, the choking
    cloud of Woodbines.

Aggie's behind the bar, or her daughter
the nun, or her son the priest taking over
as she makes dinner
for Pops and the other boarders.

The *b'Jesuses* and *begods* rising
through the smoke fill the bar, crowd out
any hope of heartfelt conversation.
But Jack winks and tries anyway,
whispering, trying to make hay with Birdie.

Old bachelor Crawford staggers over
offers nearly spilt kisses
from half pints, proposes marriage
to two American ladies, their
faces blush and brighten.

On the last stool
farthest from the light,
is Tomsy in a permanent hunch,
away from the turf bog for another day
concentrates on his pint.

Other familiar faces
are there for the serious business
of getting pissed and enjoying
the *craic* of a night out

I slip from the barroom, close the door
quietly on the shuttered past, once more.

Regret

I.

When first I came
to Letterkelly, decades back,

hundreds of rabbit warrens
were dug into the furze-

prickled slope
of Curroch O'Dea above the cottage.

How Sam Óg, the collie gave up
hunting the dying rabbits, found

no challenge in the chase.
The state took care of the rabbits

with a virus that blinded them,
then did them in.

The rabbits are gone.

II.

Six years back at Liscannor
set out on the main street,

in front of McHugh's, a coursing meet,
where the hound pursues the hare
in an enclosed run,
where gamblers throw

money at the Atlantic wind.

To bet on the hare is a dead loss
even if he outruns his pursuer.

III.

But yesterday coming back from Inagh
across from a forestry clearcut

we saw a red fox in an open meadow
looking at the valley

toward the Cullenagh River,
toward us . . .

For a moment there were red coats,
Gabriel's trumpeting

the dogs to the fox, the romance,
if you care to call it that, of the hunt.

IV.

The red fox is coming back
making up for our nostalgic loss of rabbits

but the ancient bear is a few teeth,
bones in Aillwee Cave at Ballyvaughan.
While the oak tree spread of antlers guards us
from high up on the walls of Bunratty Castle,

at the National Museum in Dublin
the Giant Irish Elk is a huge cage

of air, a skeleton.

II

Across the Distance

—for Jim Davis

My neighbour
is beginning his final journey.

A single contrail violates
the virginal sky.

I follow its path
to the long sought Polldanassa

away in Ireland at the beginning
of my first great journey.

Does the cascade falling into
the pool still sound the same?

Vague notes but I remember
golden water of the mineral yellow pool.

No hazel bush cants over it,
no nut hung ready to drop

into the mythic trout's mouth,
the fish that gave the pool its name.

Dull flat pebbles
beneath its surface

try to glitter like coins
in the weak sunlight of winter.

The Bard at Eighty

But who am I? Asks
Amergin, the first
Irish poet, standing
at The Cliffs.

I saw / was him
or ogham stone:
my hieroglyphics hard
to decipher or dimming
marks
of my ages, a blade
slicing each day
in half.

I close my eyes
sit down
amidst bog cotton
that would never make
cloth for a bard's robes,
much less a pillow.

But I lie back
full length
upon the cool cushiony
mattress, a bed
fit for a poet
even by Brehon law.

Never In Step With What Escaped Me

His hand a shaking tree
waves goodbye.

The tree, its leaves gone,
still quaking in a wind

that pulls it back
against the stone wall

like an old fairy bush,
not unlike the old man's hair

as he stands, the wall
stones loosening around him.

The gate, an old iron bedstead,
tied at the top with bailing twine

unhinges as its fibre rots away.

Who would risk wetting their ankles
crossing through the grass grown

gap to visit? It shouldn't have
been that hard for a son.

Now I go through that gap
every dream, again and again,

and stop each time to tie up the gate
with the same rotting thread.

Here, Again

On another island
between the North
and South Channels
of the Lee, watching

cars crossing Clonthard
Bridge I see
my nephew's face scarred
from fighting

battles we'll never know.
Outside suddenly
breaking into my thoughts
a sea lion surfaces

from the brown river, unlikely
this far from the sea
in the city of Cork,
but *he is* unlikely, appears

when I least expect him.
The head pops up,
then disappears, I am
hallucinating, I Think,

as his whole body breaks
the surface. He turns to me
warning me to stop
before I reveal too much

of the story.
He was my nephew,
or wasn't my half brother.
Warrior born under the sign

of water, drowned
in his own blood. . . He
comes to me in strange places,
not in dreams

but disguised
as some other creature
from the real world.

Keeping Time

The old banjo clock, heart
long since stopped.

The woman who came
to wind it gone.

The rest of time lost
from the clock's accounting

when it died in the morning
or the evening at exactly

five minutes to ten . . .

Outside, the coo-coo
in the spruce has taken up

the task of keeping time,

the interval between
its calls less precise

than the heart's tick-tock.

In late June time flies
to Scandinavia, its song lost

in high altitudes over grey Atlantic waves;
in the vagueness of flight

time keeping forgotten,
abandoned in the nest

like the coo-coo's hatch, left to chance.

"Sea-Sand"

for Dermot Healy (1947-2014)

You went back to Ballyconnell
to face again the edge of the Atlantic in Sligo.

That's the way I picture you
standing outside your poet's house
in the wind looking toward Inish Murray.

I retreated to my cottage
in Clare, where

above the turf fire
the hearth weeps.

You'd likely say
it's because of the foolish mason
who used beach sand washed in brine.

But I'd say here
a few miles inland from Atlantic breakers
on this wet dark night

the sand misses the shore,
the sea is calling back its salt.

Through the Back Window of Lost Time

Into a disused fisher's cottage,
in the gloom, the eternal light glows dim.

He needs no St Peter
to watch over, guide his days.

San Martin de Porras is enough for him.

By the front door a sea shell basin
of holy water, not from Knock

but from the sea. Rain
can be blessed why not brine?

Sprinkled with a few drops of the sea
that stung his widowed eyes

when long ago he left, turning his back
on the cabin, humming a Lenten song

in praise of *an scadán,*
the humble herring calling him away.

III

The Tenants of the World

We kiss our fingertips, touch
the mezuzah
as we leave the house.

During the evictions
the man of the house
before it was knocked,
planted a kiss
on the door post.

Each passing family
member kissed the tips of fingers
traced the outline
of the missing mezuzah.

When Irish peasants,
their families and possessions
were set out on the street . . .

and Jewish families
were driven
from the shtetl . . .

they must have known.

Achill Island

Achill, from the Latin acquila, for eagle

You can see the island
as a great bird flying
off the cliff of Ireland
into the Atlantic.

And hear at eventide
the moaning of the lost *cillíní*,
unbaptized children
in unmarked graves
outside the church wall
hidden in tidal flats,
on rocky seaside shelves.

Or catch the echo
of children's voices off Slievemore.

A local says
'Tis no more than the sea
wind whistling through the furze.

The Deserted Village

—for John McHugh of Doagh

Beneath Slievemore
a long jaw of broken
teeth, scattered ruins,
the empty village.

Evident still
the soft lazy-beds
—long grave mounds—
raised potato hills, manna
until the blight.

Listen with care
the poet says:
at twilight hear
dogs barking, playing
children's voices, keening.

The cynic says it's
the far and lost cry
sheep and their lambs,
skirling wind of the sea.

Mass Grave Near Ennistymon, Co Clare

Their blood became the rain
that nourishes this grass,
grass they tried to eat, their teeth
stained forever green, their
flesh now this piece of ground
where not even a hollow
remains to show where
the earth sucked in its belly,
tightened its straw belt
to the last notch . . .

Killaspuglonane

The mail came
from the old Post & Telegraph
in Kilshanny. The postman
on a motor bike brought it

to the stoop, letters
sometimes misdirected,
garbled telegrams, relics
of miscommunication.

I didn't want them anyway,
came here to get away.
Who would track me down
at an address in a townland

unknown to but a few?
Called *Killaspuglonane*: Church
of the Bishop Flannen
though no one knows where

the church might have been.
Behind Michael Healey's feed lot,
a holy well in the brambles,
a Famine mass grave.

Nothing but bad luck
since he built a cow barn over it.
Across the road from his farm
the Killaspuglonane Graveyard.

Up the lane at Caheraderry
no one seemed to notice
the stone crucifix atop a ruined wall.
its faint shadow flickering

in the light of the Halloween bonfire.
Uncountable ghosts, spirits, fairies,
and púcas inhabit the parish
despite all the crosses.

They didn't disturb my dreams
when I spent a wet winter there,
burnt up a rick of turf, writing and
sleeping peaceful hours

comforted by my own protecting púca,
wet and shivering, as he passed
on his usual path like a sentry
at the west gable end of the cottage,

as the wailing southwest wind, louder than
banshees, from the Atlantic
drove pellets of icy rain
against the window.

Nightboat

Leaving Rosslare astern
cottage hurricane lamps dim
to faltering pin pricks of light.

Over an abandoned country
stars fall like sparks
as the wind shakes out
the blanket of the night.

Ballygowan

He hadn't a coin to flip
but turned the flat pebble
again and again hoping
to uncover the suggestion

of a head *Damn*
the new king anyway
his hated name . . .
In disgust he sailed

the thin stone, watched it
arc into the wet wind
over rock walls and furze.
Ahead of him the tang of the near sea

as he walked out of
his brogues, bare heels
red to the weather but
hob nails kept shiny

from the travelling.
He walked away, ankles
worn raw from turf
and limestone dust,

from the town, imagined a spot
along a track called Gowan's.
He trudged on, sea sting
in his nostrils, dreaming

the taste of a pinch of salt
on a boiled pratty. Like the one
he stole from the lazy bed
too near the road, carried hidden

like a plague bump beneath his coat.
Years hence on the other side, they
asked him where he was from,
Ireland he mumbled into his chin.

Where in Ireland? *Begod
T'was Ballygowan*, the last name
he remembered before he shipped,
or else it wasn't.

IV

Trespass

We dug out a spring at the base of Curroch O'Dea
after our neighbor from Mount Callan,
with a willow fork as a dowsing rod, found water.

But even in my dreams I was never able
to find the spring again, once the cows left it,
once the plantation of Sitka spruce took over.

The once furze covered slope
blanketed by another invasion covering
a bog hole that was Jack Dan's old well.

We never used it, drank instead
from water hidden in the trees by the lane
that leads to the abandoned cottage.

We left it like we left the pool,
the pitiful twist of wire
hardly kept out trespassing cows;

nor the collapsing haggard gate
we posted to keep out others,
corroded by the invisible intruder.

You'd only to taste your lips
to know he was there,
crossing your bounds.

Tottenham's Trees

By the small pool stands
an oak sapling planted by God

knows who . . . Ireland was once
covered with oak forests,

and beech, sycamore, before
the English came, took

"the English oak"
for flotillas, for antique furniture.

Now the marshes are green,
another invader, Sitka spruce.

We can't keep up with the evergreens
blanketing the hills, the bogs, but

no matter who planted them they'll
come down as fenceposts, pulp, and timber.

Where trees once stood
black bog again, its cotton waving.

According to Pakie Russell

Joe Dowling, Casement's emissary, in 1916
is mistakenly dropped on Crab Island,
the submarine commander
thinking it the mainland . . .

As the U-boat disappears in midnight fog
Joe realizes he's 500 yds from shore
but swim he must the dark waters,
Pakie is watching at Doolin Quay to take his hand
to pull him from the water . . .

I'd heard these stories time
and time again when Pakie put aside
the concertina, took a right healthy pull
from his pint of the dark stuff, began to yarn . . .

Some nights it's Casement
himself who lands, though book history
says Sir Roger came ashore
south of the Shannon on Banna Beach in Tralee Bay.

Whatever was in it you can be sure Pakie is there
giving his hero the ole IRA salute . . .

I sat listening to Pakie
fuelling his enthusiasm with pints of Guinness
but alas too often before he was half way through
the tape rewound:

. . .the German sub is again surfacing
on the lee side of Crab Island
ready to drop off its IRA emissary

Eager for some forgotten detail
my ears attended every telling
and re-telling of his tales of intrigue
though often he never finished.

I was plenty willing to supply the liquid
inspiration for Pakie, seanchaí of Fisher Street,
to keep him talking, his tales more interesting
than his concertina playing.

Just before Gussie O'Connor rang the bell
for last call, sang out "Now gents . . . Time. . ."

> Joe Dowling, black beret pulled down over his right eye,
> forehead sweating, sneaks into the side door
> by the shop counter, not bothering to stop
> long enough to buy a few extra bottles
> of porter for after last call, his cat eyes
> searching for his biographer,
> and a few pints or two for his story

But it's Rory, face as red as a lantern,
who cruises the long bar, sidles
up to a table, offering a whisper, just a possibility
a bottle
of the best poteen
along the coast.

A Clare Story

"Our Lady of the Telephone Booth,"
Brigid by the roadside out of Lahinch
up the incline towards The Cliffs
just before O'Brien's monument and the pub.

*

The parade of cars
coming up the hill endless
all the way up the coast from Miltown.

Don't you see
as I drove up the grade
Half awake and missing my tea,

she turned and winked
from the glass enclosure.

Had I blinked I would have missed it.

I couldn't believe what I'd seen.
It rattled me. A drink
was what I needed.

I pulled in at the near pub,

had to tell the publican,

who gave me a look,
went straight to phone.

Life, And A Pine Marten

In 1790 the Harans raised the
three feet thick rock walls,

thatched the roof
of the little cottage on the bog

beneath Currach O'Dea,
a quiet place the neighbors said—

and left the rest to us, when
we bought it, and moved in, in 1972.

We soon had it done up, washed
white, with blue barge boards,

a bright red door clearly
visible from the county road,

and smoke from the chimney,
our calling card, told the folks

around Letterkelly and Cloonanaha
the Yankee man was back.

It was rustic: floor, Liscannor
flags, a hearth the only heat.

Kindly neighbors
gave us peat a plenty to burn.

As I piled the sods of turf on the fire
we built a life in that cottage.

II.

But when snow flakes fell
between us and on Mt Callan

it was mighty cold,
hard to get the fire going,

easier to let it die out, leave
but ashes in the hearth.

III.

The last time I slept in the cottage
a pine marten in the attic

kept me awake chewing up
sheets of styrofoam we'd put

in the rafters for insulation,
making himself a future home.

I got out of bed
took a broom handle

to the ceiling boards
—my thumping scared him away.

But the pine marten
moved in to stay.

Now there's a forest
grown up around the place.

The woman who built
a life with me there

no longer returned.

With Ireland it wasn't
so much a divorce as a separation.

I lost heart,
didn't come home for a time.

When I did it was just me
and the pine marten.

I couldn't put up with the racket
so I left the cottage to him

and I was left with the guilt
of leaving.

Memory Stone

—for stonemasons, for Paddy

The hands
the sweat
the broken thumb,
the blister forming

secretly in the glove.
The scarred knuckle,
the explosion
when steel meets stone.

The stars
we see
from lifting.
The daily ache,

soul of stone
dust we wash
away from
hands revealing

scars
we count like years.

A Song for St Paddy's

I am about to cross another border
to bridge a stream
that threads through eight decades.

The other border is less grievous
from one country to Ireland
if I ignore the clock, the year

when someone will lead me
blindfolded across the bog that is Erin
where I will put my ear to the earth
like Finn McCool.

I may not hear the rumble
the falls above the Pool
of the Trout but I will yet feel
its seismic heart beating . . .

already has me thinking
of my next meandering
across the green, the lime-
stone face of Ireland.

Photograph by Karen Checkoway

Poet and translator CARLOS REYES first came to Ireland in the early 1970s, when he purchased a three-hundred-year-old cottage in County Clare. His neighbors in Letterkelly consider him part of the family. For 40 years, Reyes was publisher and editor of Trask House Books, a poetry press. He is a founding editor of *Hubbub*, a poetry magazine, and served on the editorial staff of *Ar Mhuin na Muice (On a Pigs Back)*, an Irish literary journal. He has published ten volumes of poetry, many volumes of translations, and a memoir, *Keys to the Cottage, Stories from the West of Ireland* (2015). His most recent poetry book is *Guilt in Our Pockets, Poems from South India* (2017). He is the recipient of a Heinrich Böll Fellowship (Achill Island, Ireland) and fellowships from Yaddo and the Fundación Valparaíso (Mojácar, Spain). Acadia National Park and Joshua Tree National Park among others have hosted him where he has served as poet-in-residence. When not traveling, Reyes makes his home in Portland, Oregon USA.

2 1982 03019 7945

www.**salmon**poetry.com

*"Like the sea-run Steelhead salmon that thrashes upstream to its spawning
ground, then instead of dying, returns to the sea – Salmon Poetry Press
brings precious cargo to both Ireland and America in the poetry it publishes,
then carries that select work to its readership against incalculable odds."*

TESS GALLAGHER